To Angel,
With much love

Judy
8-20-12

DAILY STRENGTHS
FOR DAILY NEEDS

First published by Parragon in 2009

Parragon
Queen Street House
4 Queen Street
Bath BA1 1HE, UK

Copyright © Parragon Books Ltd 2009
Design by Pink Creative Ltd

ISBN: 978-1-4075-8644-1

Printed in China

DAILY STRENGTHS
FOR DAILY NEEDS

A COLLECTION OF MOTIVATIONAL
QUOTES AND IMAGES

Bath · New York · Singapore · Hong Kong · Cologne · Delhi · Melbourne

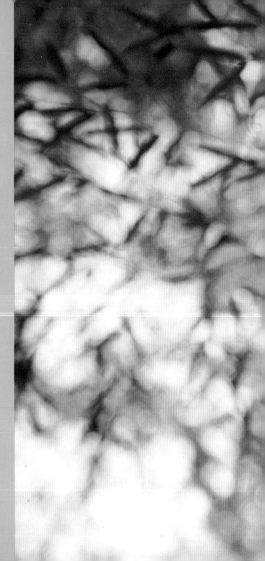

Early to bed and early to rise makes a man

healthy,

wealthy,

and **wise.**

Benjamin Franklin,
One of the Founding Fathers of the United
States of America.

Make the most of yourself, for that is all there is of you.

Ralph Waldo Emerson,
Essayist, philosopher and poet

A gentle breeze

blowing in the right direction

is better than a pair

of strong oars.

Canary Island proverb

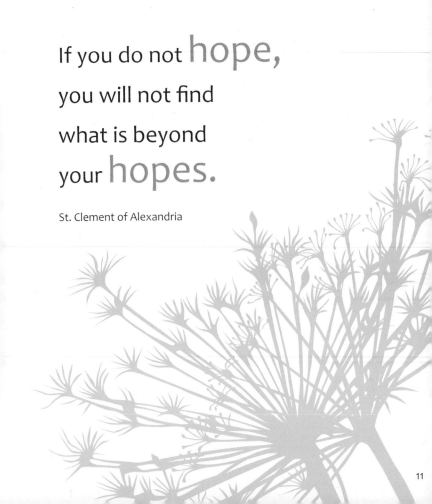

If you do not hope,
you will not find
what is beyond
your hopes.

St. Clement of Alexandria

A strong person and a waterfall
always channel their own path.

Unknown

We are still **masters** of our fate.

We are still **captains** of our souls.

Winston Churchill, Former British Prime Minister

Happiness is when what you think, what you say, and what you do are in harmony.

Mahatma Gandhi, political and spiritual leader of India

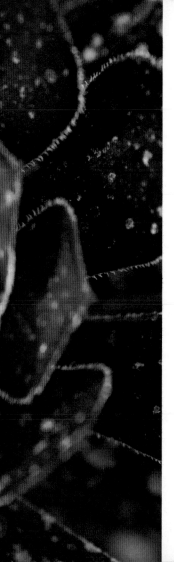

Be not afraid
of growing slowly,
be afraid only
of standing still.

Chinese proverb

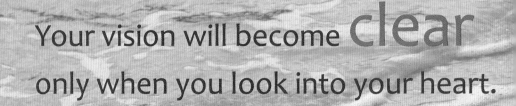

Your vision will become clear only when you look into your heart.

Who looks outside, dreams.

Who looks inside, awakens.

Carl Gustav Jung, Psychiatrist

Life is not measured
by the breaths we take,
but by the moments
that take our breath.

Unknown

23

The best and most **beautiful things** in the world cannot be seen or even touched.

They must be felt with the heart.

Hellen Keller, Author, political activist and lecturer

Don't judge

those who try and fail,

judge those

who fail to try.

Unknown

Never look down on anyone unless you're helping him up.

Jesse Jackson,
American Civil rights activist
and Baptist minister

No act of **kindness,**

however small,

is ever wasted.

Unknown

A pessimist
sees the difficulty in every opportunity;

an optimist
sees the opportunity in every difficulty.

Unknown

Happiness depends on what you can give. Not what you can get.

Mahatma Gandhi, political and spiritual leader of India

Think of all
the beauty
still left
around you
and be happy.

Anne Frank,
German diarist and fugitive of the Third Reich

The more light
you allow within you,

the brighter the world
you live in will be.

Shakti Gawain, Author

Never live
in the past

but always
learn from it.

Unknown

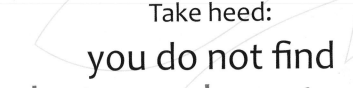

Take heed:
you do not find
what you do not seek.

Proverb

Pull the string,

and it will follow

wherever you wish.

Push it, and it will go

nowhere at all.

Dwight D. Eisenhower, Former President
of the United States of America

He who lives
in harmony with himself
lives in harmony
with the world.

Marcus Aurelius, Roman Emperor

Things today **may not be great,** but they are not bad, **and that's good.**

Unknown

There are only two ways to live your life. One is as though nothing is a miracle. The other is as though everything is a miracle.

Albert Einstein, German physicist

A life spent making mistakes is not only

more honourable,

but more useful

than a life spent doing nothing.

George Bernard Shaw, British playwright

We make
a living
by what
we get,
we make
a life
by what
we give.

Winston Churchill, Former British Prime Minister

Let us be grateful to people who make us happy;

they are the charming gardeners who make our souls blossom.

Marcel Proust, French novelist

Courage doesn't always roar.
Sometimes courage is
the quiet voice
at the end of the day saying,
"I will try again tomorrow."

Mary Anne Radmacher, Author

Failure is taking the path that everyone else does, success is making your own path.

Unknown

Life isn't about **finding** yourself.

Life is about creating yourself.

George Bernard Shaw, British playwright

Imagination will often carry us to worlds that never were.
But without it we go nowhere.

Carl Sagan, Astronomer

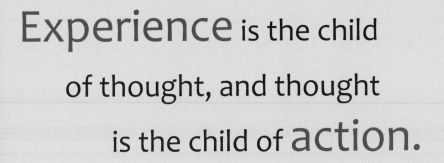

Experience is the child of thought, and thought is the child of action.

Benjamin Disraeli, Former British Prime Minister

What you see depends on
what you're looking for.

Unknown

Teach us delight
in simple things,
and mirth that has
no bitter springs.

Rudyard Kipling, British author and poet

What lies behind us

and what lies before us

are tiny matters compared

to what lies within us.

Walt Emerson, Artist and educator

There is no greatness
where there is not simplicity.

Leo Tolstoy, Russian novelist

With the new day comes

new strengths and new thoughts

Eleanor Roosevelt, Former First Lady of the United States of America

Peace comes from within.
Do not seek it without it.

Gautama Siddharta, Buddha Spiritual leader

Be **faithful** in small things

because it is in them

that your **strength lies.**

Mother Teresa, Roman Catholic Nun and humanitarian

Anyone who has never made a mistake has never tried anything new.

Albert Einstein, German physicist

Anyone can hold the helm

when the sea is calm.

Unknown

He who hesitates

is lost.

Proverb

In seed time learn,

in harvest teach,

in winter enjoy.

William Blake, British poet

Confidence comes not from

always being right,

but from not fearing

to be wrong.

Unknown

Everything you do
can be done better
from a place of relaxation.

Stephen C Paul, Writer

Have regular hours for work and play;
make each day both useful and pleasant,
and prove that you understand the worth
if time by employing it well.

Then youth will be delightful,
old age will bring few regrets and life
will become a beautiful success,
in spite of poverty.

Louise May Alcott, Author of *Little Women*

Picture credits